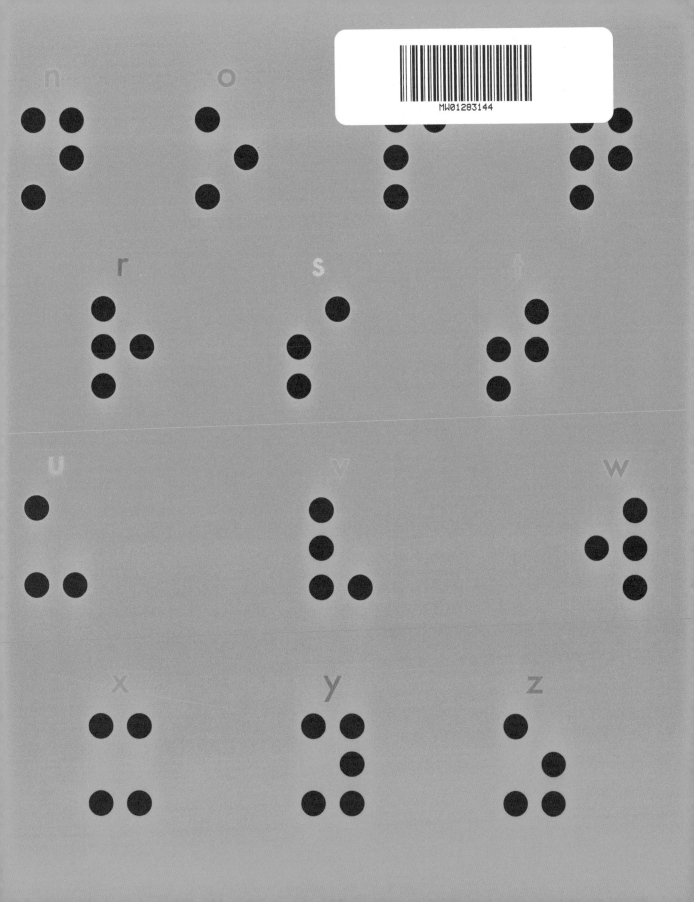

Little People, BIG DREAMS™

LOUIS BRAILLE

Written by
Maria Isabel Sánchez Vegara

Illustrated by
Ana Albero

Frances Lincoln
Children's Books

Monsieur and Madame Braille lived in a village near Paris, France. They had four children, and their youngest, Louis, was the most adventurous. As soon as he could walk, his dad's workshop became his favorite place to explore.

When he was three, Louis had an accident while playing with his father's tools and injured his eye.

It became infected, and the infection spread to his other eye, too. By the time he was five, he was completely blind.

His new life was hard to get used to, but it didn't stop him! Louis learned the alphabet by feeling letters made with nails on a wooden board. Soon after, a family friend, Father Palluy, convinced the village teacher to let Louis join the local school.

Like many people at the time, his teacher thought that children needed to see to be able to learn. Still, it was just a matter of time before Louis proved that was wrong. He couldn't read the blackboard, but he could use his mind!

At ten, Louis earned a spot at the world's first school for blind boys, in Paris. He imagined it would be a place with all the tools he needed to read, write, and play music. Sadly, his excitement would soon turn to disappointment.

The school had very few books, which were written using a tricky system. To read just a word, Louis had to run his fingers slowly over the big, raised letters. Reading sentences took a lot of effort, and . . . it couldn't even be used to write!

One day, a captain in the French army visited Louis' school. He had created a system of raised dots that soldiers used to read and write in the dark. All they needed was a simple board and a pocket-sized stamp. Louis couldn't wait to try it!

The new system was better, but still tricky. It used a box with twelve dots to make shapes that stood for sounds, not letters like A, B, or C. The dots were so far apart that readers had to use almost their whole finger to feel them. Many gave up, but not Louis!

Over the next four years, he improved the system. Louis made a smaller box with six bumps that fit neatly under his fingertip. Instead of using sounds, he gave every letter its own pattern of raised dots. It was easier to learn and use in any language!

Louis was only sixteen when he showed his system to his classmates and teachers. They were excited to try it, and amazed at how quickly they could read and write not only letters, but also numbers and punctuation marks.

Three years later, Louis went from being a student to a teacher. He taught math, history, geography, grammar, and music.

Even with all that, he still found time to add musical notes to his system. He loved playing different instruments!

It took a long time for his writing system to be used outside of the school. By then, Louis was no longer there, but he was still remembered. As the system spread from place to place, people started calling it "Braille" to honor its inventor.

Today, millions of people use their fingertips and the Braille system to read, write, and discover amazing new things. And it's all because of little Louis, the boy who turned a few dots and a simple idea into a gift for the world.

LOUIS BRAILLE

(Born 1809 – Died 1852)

1843   c. 1850s

Louis Braille was born in 1809 in a village in France. When he was three years old, he injured his eye in an accident. By the age of five, he had lost his sight completely. Growing up blind at that time was not easy, but Louis had a brilliant mind and a loving family. At ten, he won a scholarship to the Royal Institute for Blind Youth in Paris. The few books there were printed with big raised letters, which students traced with their fingers. Reading it was difficult and slow—by the time children reached the end of a sentence, they sometimes couldn't remember how it had started! In 1821, an army captain named Charles Barbier de la Serre visited the institute to share a new reading system he had developed. Instead of using raised letters, it used different combinations of raised dots to represent the different

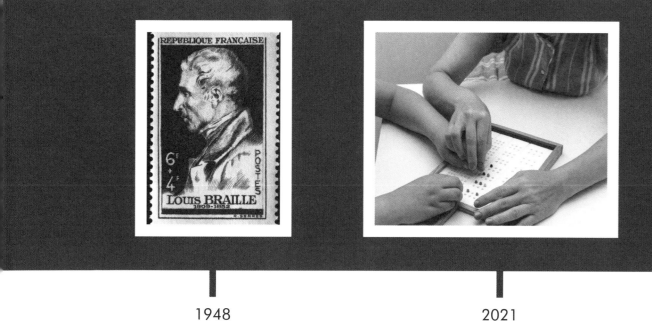

1948   2021

sounds that make up letters. Barbier's code made reading easier, but it wasn't perfect, so twelve-year-old Louis decided to redesign it! Four years later, he shared his own system, which used a simple six-dot code to represent letters, numbers, and punctuation marks. The code could be adapted to work for different languages, mathematical symbols, and even for writing music. It was an amazing achievement. Louis stayed on at the institute for most of his life, teaching students and perfecting his code. It was only after his death that his invention began to spread beyond the institute and around the world. Today, there are Braille codes for over 130 languages. Every year on January 4th, Louis' birthday, World Braille Day celebrates the remarkable man who changed the lives of millions.

Want to find out more?

Have a read of this great book:

Who Was Louis Braille? by Margaret Frith

To my dear Arthur, may your dreams take you far.

Text © 2025 Maria Isabel Sánchez Vegara. Illustrations © 2025 Ana Albero.
Original idea of the series by Maria Isabel Sánchez Vegara, published by Alba Editorial, s.l.u.
"Little People, BIG DREAMS" and "Pequeña & Grande" are trademarks of
Alba Editorial S.L.U. and/or Beautifool Couple S.L.
First published in the US in 2025 by Frances Lincoln Children's Books, an imprint of The Quarto Group.
Quarto Boston North Shore, 100 Cummings Center, Suite 265D, Beverly, MA 01915, USA
Tel: +1 978-282-9590 **www.Quarto.com**
EEA Representation, WTS Tax d.o.o., Žanova ulica 3, 4000 Kranj, Slovenia.

A CIP record for this book is available from the Library of Congress.
ISBN 978-1-83600-741-8
Set in Futura BT.
Published by Peter Marley · Edited by Molly Mead
Designed by Sasha Moxon and Izzy Bowman
Production by Robin Boothroyd
Manufactured in Guangdong, China CC052025
1 3 5 7 9 8 6 4 2

Photographic acknowledgments (pages 28–29, from left to right): 1. Royal Institution for blind youth building in Paris, published
on Magasin Pittoresque, 1843 © Oldtime via Alamy Stock Photo. 2. Louis Braille (1809-1852). French teacher of the blind.
Undated lithograph after a daguerreotype taken shortly after his death in 1852 © Granger—Historical Picture Archive / Granger NYC
via Alamy Stock Photo. 3. Louis Braille, postage stamp, France, 1948 © Ivan Vdovin via Alamy Stock Photo. 4. The hands of
a girl and the hands of a teacher in close-up. Braille board for learning alphabet © Predrag Lasica via Alamy Stock Photo.

MIX
Paper | Supporting
responsible forestry
FSC® C008047

Collect the *Little People*, **BIG DREAMS**™ series:

FRIDA KAHLO · COCO CHANEL · MAYA ANGELOU · AMELIA EARHART · AGATHA CHRISTIE · MARIE CURIE · ROSA PARKS · AUDREY HEPBURN · EMMELINE PANKHURST

ELLA FITZGERALD · ADA LOVELACE · JANE AUSTEN · GEORGIA O'KEEFFE · HARRIET TUBMAN · ANNE FRANK · MOTHER TERESA · JOSEPHINE BAKER · L. M. MONTGOMERY

JANE GOODALL · SIMONE DE BEAUVOIR · MUHAMMAD ALI · STEPHEN HAWKING · MARIA MONTESSORI · VIVIENNE WESTWOOD · MAHATMA GANDHI · DAVID BOWIE · WILMA RUDOLPH

DOLLY PARTON · BRUCE LEE · RUDOLF NUREYEV · ZAHA HADID · MARY SHELLEY · MARTIN LUTHER KING JR. · DAVID ATTENBOROUGH · ASTRID LINDGREN · EVONNE GOOLAGONG

BOB DYLAN · ALAN TURING · BILLIE JEAN KING · GRETA THUNBERG · JESSE OWENS · JEAN-MICHEL BASQUIAT · ARETHA FRANKLIN · CORAZON AQUINO · PELÉ

ERNEST SHACKLETON · STEVE JOBS · AYRTON SENNA · LOUISE BOURGEOIS · ELTON JOHN · JOHN LENNON · PRINCE · CHARLES DARWIN · CAPTAIN TOM MOORE

HANS CHRISTIAN ANDERSEN · STEVIE WONDER · MEGAN RAPINOE · MARY ANNING · MALALA YOUSAFZAI · ANDY WARHOL · RUPAUL · MICHELLE OBAMA · MINDY KALING

IRIS APFEL · ROSALIND FRANKLIN · RUTH BADER GINSBURG · MARILYN MONROE · KAMALA HARRIS · ALBERT EINSTEIN · CHARLES DICKENS · YOKO ONO · MICHAEL JORDAN

| NELSON MANDELA | PABLO PICASSO | AMANDA GORMAN | GLORIA STEINEM | FLORENCE NIGHTINGALE | HARRY HOUDINI | J.R.R. TOLKIEN | ELVIS PRESLEY | NEIL ARMSTRONG |

| ALEXANDER VON HUMBOLDT | NIKOLA TESLA | WILMA MANKILLER | MARCUS RASHFORD | LAVERNE COX | MAE JEMISON | DWAYNE JOHNSON | HELEN KELLER | ANNA PAVLOVA |

| QUEEN ELIZABETH | TERRY FOX | HEDY LAMARR | SHAKIRA | FREDDIE MERCURY | LEWIS HAMILTON | LOUIS PASTEUR | PRINCESS DIANA | DAVID HOCKNEY |

| VANESSA NAKATE | OLIVE MORRIS | KING CHARLES | MOZART | STEVE IRWIN | JÜRGEN KLOPP | LEO MESSI | SALLY RIDE | TENZING NORGAY |

| KYLIE MINOGUE | BEYONCÉ | TAYLOR SWIFT | RAFA NADAL | USAIN BOLT | SIMONE BILES | STAN LEE | LEONARD COHEN | VINCENT VAN GOGH |

| MARY KOM | SALVADOR DALÍ | ANTOINE DE SAINT-EXUPÉRY | DAVID BECKHAM | KATHERINE JOHNSON | PATRICK MAHOMES |

| YAYOI KUSAMA | ROALD DAHL | HARRY STYLES | WILLIAM KAMKWAMBA | MARY EARPS | YVES SAINT LAURENT |

| BOB MARLEY | VIRGINIA WOOLF | LUDWIG VAN BEETHOVEN | LOUIS BRAILLE |

Scan the QR code for free activity sheets, teachers' notes and more information about the series at www.littlepeoplebigdreams.com

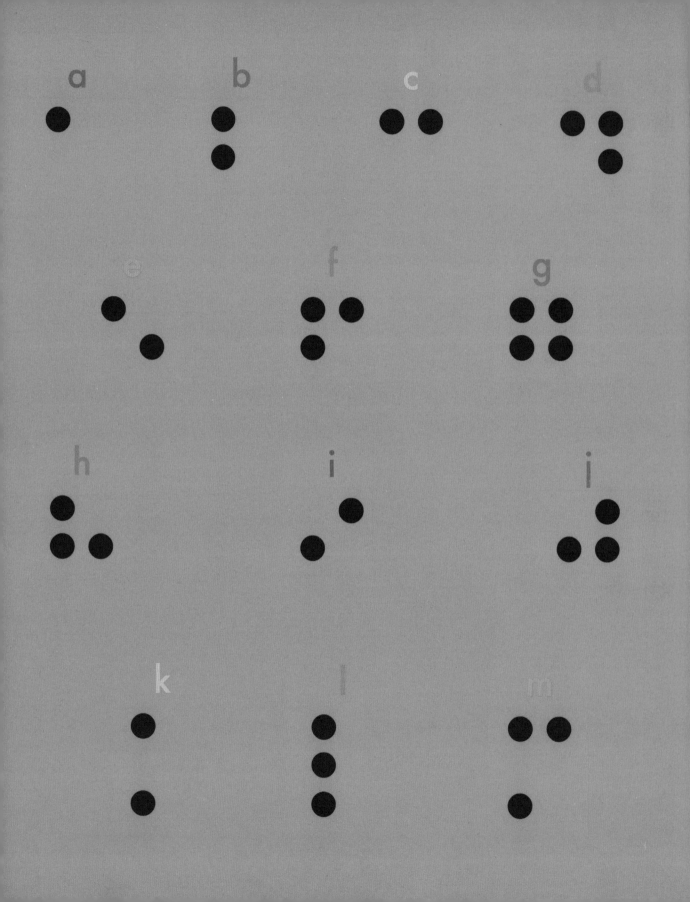